NO LONGER THE PROPERTY OF THE
DENVER PUBLIC LIBRARY

Let's Explore Kenya

by Elle Parkes

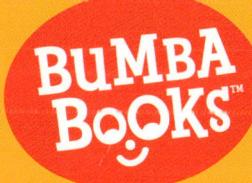

BUMBA BOOKS™

LERNER PUBLICATIONS ◆ MINNEAPOLIS

DENVER PUBLIC LIBRARY

Note to Educators:

Throughout this book, you'll find critical thinking questions. These can be used to engage young readers in thinking critically about the topic and in using the text and photos to do so.

Copyright © 2018 by Lerner Publishing Group, Inc.

All rights reserved. International copyright secured. No part of this book may be reproduced, stored in a retrieval system, or transmitted in any form or by any means—electronic, mechanical, photocopying, recording, or otherwise—without the prior written permission of Lerner Publishing Group, Inc., except for the inclusion of brief quotations in an acknowledged review.

Lerner Publications Company
A division of Lerner Publishing Group, Inc.
241 First Avenue North
Minneapolis, MN 55401 USA

For reading levels and more information, look up this title at www.lernerbooks.com.

Library of Congress Cataloging-in-Publication Data

Names: Parkes, Elle, author.
Title: Let's explore Kenya / by Elle Parkes.
Other titles: Let's explore countries.
Description: Minneapolis : Lerner Publications, 2017. | Series: Let's explore countries | Includes bibliographical references and index.
Identifiers: LCCN 2016042315 (print) | LCCN2016042813 (ebook) | ISBN 9781512433647 (lb : alk. paper) | ISBN 9781512455601 (pb) | ISBN 9781512450408 (eb pdf)
Subjects: LCSH: Kenya—Juvenile literature.
Classification: LCC DT433.522 .P375 2017 (print) | LCC DT433.522 (ebook) | DDC 967.62—dc23

LC record available at https://lccn.loc.gov/2016042315

Manufactured in the United States of America
1 — CG — 7/15/17

Expand learning beyond the printed book. Download free, complementary educational resources for this book from our website, www.lernerresource.com.

Table of Contents

A Visit to Kenya 4

Map of Kenya 22

Picture Glossary 23

Read More 24

Index 24

A Visit to Kenya

Kenya is a country.

It is in Africa.

Kenya is next to the ocean.

It has sandy beaches.

The country has dry deserts too.

There are grasslands in Kenya.
Zebras live in Kenya's grasslands.

What do you think zebras in the grasslands eat?

Kenya also has many kinds of forests.

Elephants roam in the rain forest.

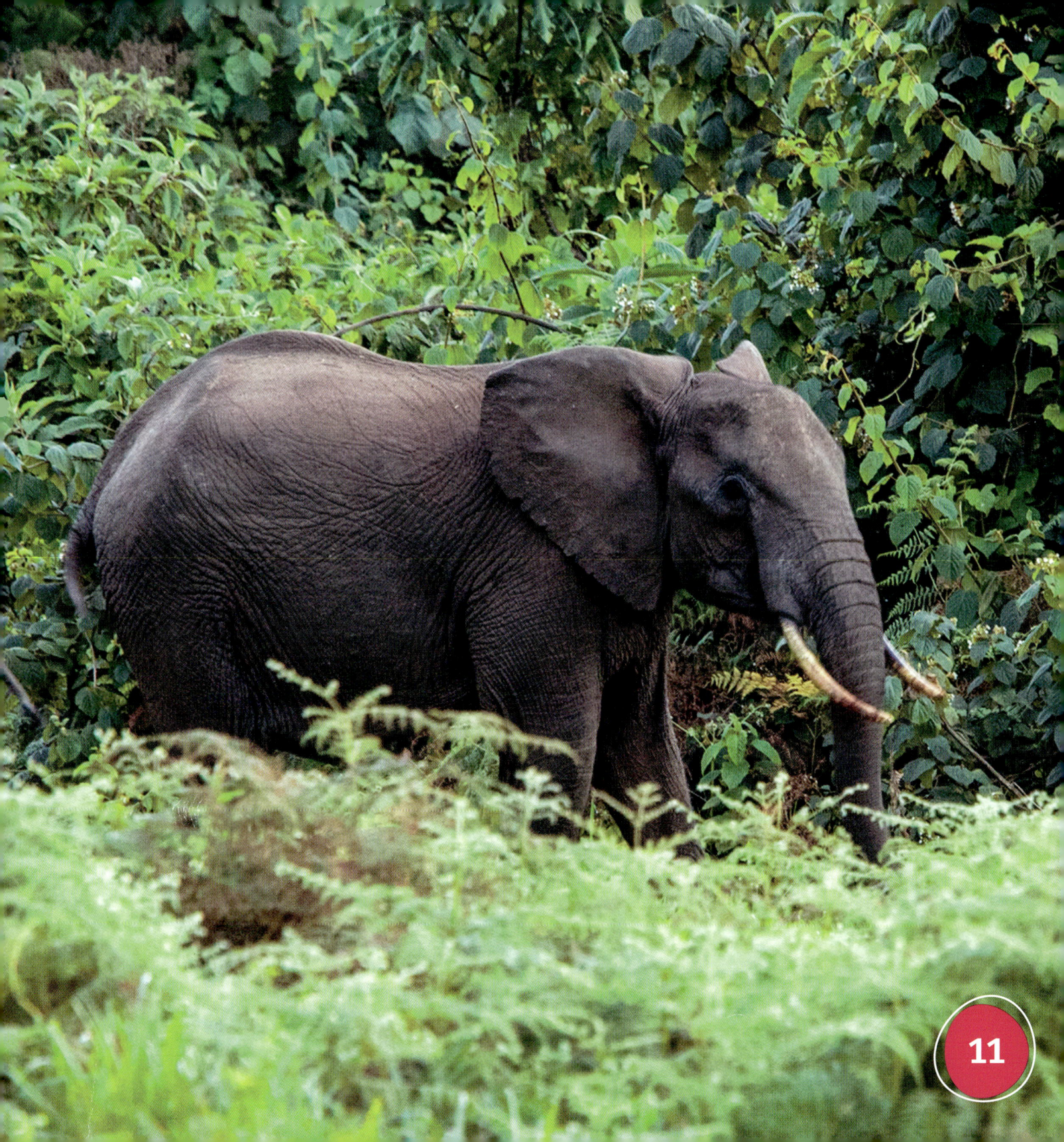

Kenya has big cities.

Nairobi is the biggest.

Many people live in Nairobi.

Other people live in

small towns.

People travel to Kenya.

They visit forests and grasslands.

They see lions.

What other animals do you think people see in Kenya?

There are a lot of fruits that grow in Kenya.

People buy fruits at markets.

What kind of fruits do you think people in Kenya buy at markets?

Mancala is a popular game in Kenya.

It is played with two people.

Players move rocks or beads around a board.

Kenya is a beautiful country.

There are many things to see.

Would you like to go to Kenya?

Map of Kenya

- desert
- rain forest
- Kenya
- Nairobi
- grassland
- ocean

Picture Glossary

grasslands

places where land is covered in grasses and other small plants

mancala

a game played with two people, a board, and rocks or beads

markets

outdoor shops where people can buy things like fresh fruits

rain forests

thick, tropical forests where lots of rain falls

Read More

Hirsch, Rebecca E. *Africa*. New York: Children's Press, 2013.

Lindeen, Mary. *Elephants*. Minneapolis: Jump!, 2014.

Parkes, Elle. *Let's Explore Haiti*. Minneapolis: Lerner Publications, 2018.

Index

deserts, 6

elephants, 10

grasslands, 9, 14

lions, 14

mancala, 18

markets, 17

Nairobi, 13

rain forest, 10

zebras, 9

Photo Credits

The images in this book are used with the permission of: © PHOTOCREO Michal Bednarek/Shutterstock.com, p. 5; © George Clerk/iStock.com, pp. 6–7; © lucagal/iStock.com, pp. 8–9, 23 (top left); © John Wollwerth/Shutterstock.com, pp. 11, 23 (bottom right); © Authentic travel/Shutterstock.com, pp. 12–13; © Josef Friedhuber/iStock.com, pp. 14–15; © Aleksandar Todorovic/Shutterstock.com, pp. 16, 23 (bottom left); © Papa Bravo/Shutterstock.com, pp. 18–19, 23 (top right); © Anna Omelchenko/Shutterstock.com, p. 20; © Red Line Editorial, p. 22.

Front Cover: © oversnap/iStock.com.